FERRETS

WEIRD PETS

Lynn M. Stone

Rourke Publishing LLC
Vero Beach, Florida 32964

www.rourkepublishing.com

PHOTO CREDITS:
All photos © Lynn M. Stone except pages 7, 12, 15 ©Novia Behling

EDITORIAL SERVICES:
Pamela Schroeder

Library of Congress Cataloging-in-Publication Data

Stone, Lynn M.
    Ferrets / Lynn M. Stone
       p. cm — (Weird Pets)
    ISBN 1-58952-038-6
      1.Ferrets as pets—Juvenile literature [1. Ferrets as pets. 2. Pets.]
      I.Title.

SF459.F47 S76 2001
636.9'76628—dc21   00-054285

Printed in the USA

TABLE OF CONTENTS

WEASELS

People own many different kinds of unusual pets—even weasels! You may even know someone with a pet weasel. If you know someone with a ferret, you know someone with a weasel.

Domestic, or tame, ferrets are one of many kinds of weasels. Weasels belong to the same group of furry, meat-eating animals as skunks, badgers, otters, martens, and fishers.

A wild short-tailed weasel looks like a mini ferret.

The domestic ferret's **ancestors** were wild weasels in Europe. They were called polecats. The black-footed ferret is a very rare weasel of the western United States.

Wild weasels are known for being quick, nervous, and fierce. They are very good at killing **prey**. A wild weasel's prey may be mice, rats, birds, rabbits, or other small animals. Because of their long, snaky bodies, weasels love to hunt in **burrows**.

6

This baby ferret was born with a love for running into and out of holes, just like its wild ancestors.

Domestic ferrets act differently than their wild cousins. Ferrets have been raised in homes for at least 2,400 years. The first ferret owners used their animals to kill mice and rats. Ferrets were also used to chase rabbits from their burrows.

Domestic ferrets are very active. They are not as fierce as wild ferrets. They enjoy being held, and they love to nap.

Ferrets nap in the bunk beds inside their travel cage.

Domestic ferrets look much like their wild cousins, except in fur color. Wild European polecats are mostly brown. The American Ferret Association lists 12 different colors of domestic ferrets.

Ferrets come in many colors, including pure white.

Ferrets can catch many diseases, but they often live from 5 to 7 years.

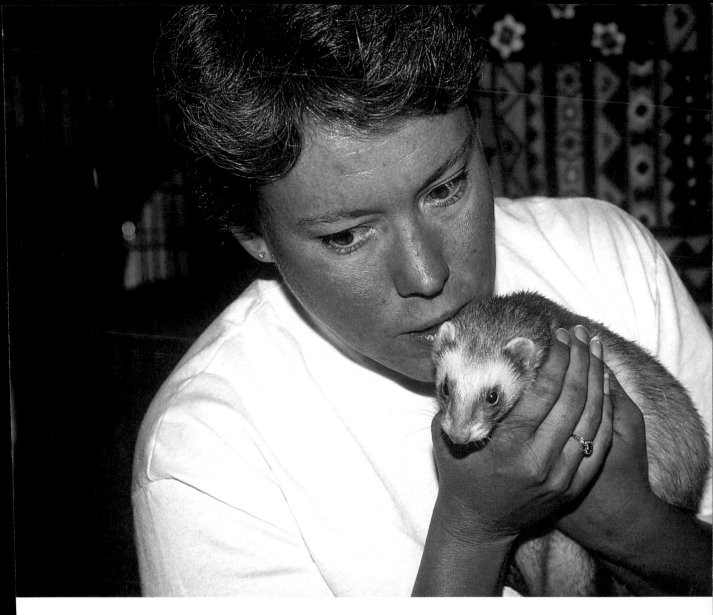

Fluffy ferrets enjoy being held, but they have sharp teeth and can bite.

FERRETS: PET FRIENDLY?

A ferret can be a great pet for anyone who has time and patience. Being a ferret owner is not an easy job.

Ferrets are playful, cuddly, and curious. They're quiet and they love their naps. Most of them can be trained to use a litter box, too.

Many owners take their ferrets to shows run by the American Ferret Association or other clubs.

Most ferrets can be trained to use a litter box.

Many people with pet ferrets, though, soon give them up. Ferret rescue groups run **shelters**. Shelters are places that keep and care for unwanted ferrets.

People give up their ferrets for many reasons. One reason is mischief. Ferrets need exercise time outside their cages. But, a ferret outside its cage will find mischief. The ferret may dig into house plants or chew on toys and shoes. It may dig under the carpet.

Judges at a show check out a ferret.

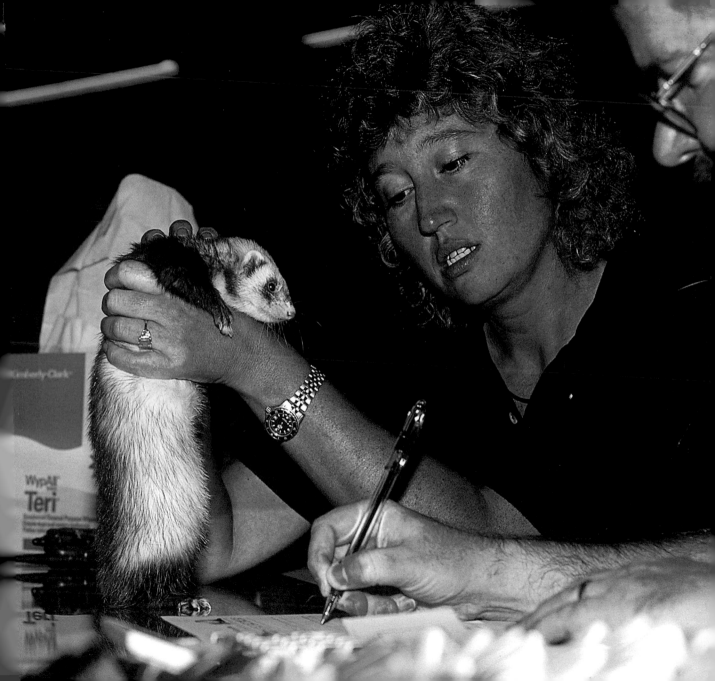

Another problem with some ferrets is their scent, or smell. Like other members of the weasel family, ferrets have powerful scent glands. Domestic ferrets don't often spray their scent, but it lasts a long time when they do.

Ferrets don't often bite, either. But, they can and sometimes do. Small children should never handle ferrets. It's safer that way for both the children and the ferrets.

Ferrets love to slip into small places, even sweater sleeves.

CARING FOR FERRETS

A ferret needs hands-on care. It needs a good cage, water, safe toys, a litter box, and a place to sleep. Ferrets like to curl up in an old stocking cap, shirt, or towel.

Ferrets can have cages outdoors or be taken out for exercise.

Ferrets can catch many diseases. Having a **veterinarian**, or animal doctor, nearby is important.

Ferrets should be fed a high quality dry food. Good dry food may look like cereal, but it's made of animal products.

GLOSSARY

ancestor (AN ses ter) — relatives of an animal that lived in the past

burrow (BUR oh) — a hole or tunnel an animal digs into the ground

domestic (deh MES tik) — refers to a type of animal that has been kept by people and tamed for many years, perhaps thousands

prey (PRAY) — an animal that is hunted by another animal for food

shelter (SHEL ter) — a place where unwanted pets are given care

veterinarian (vet er eh NAYR ee en) — an animal doctor

INDEX

Further Reading

Stone, Lynn. *Weasels*. Rourke Publishing, 1995
Gelman, Amy. *My Pet Ferret*. Lerner, 2000

Websites To Visit

•www.ferret.org   •www.gcfa.com

About The Author

Lynn Stone is the author of over 400 children's books. He is a talented natural history photographer as well. Lynn, a former teacher, travels worldwide to photograph wildlife in their natural habitat.